THE FIRST BOOK OF DRAWING

PICTURE CREDITS

The FIRST BOOK of
DRAWING

by LOUIS SLOBODKIN

SBN 531-00516-X
Library of Congress Catalog Card Number: 58-11352
© Copyright 1958 by Louis Slobodkin

Printed in the United States of America
Published in Canada by Ambassador Books, Ltd., Toronto 1, Ontario

20

FRANKLIN WATTS | NEW YORK | LONDON

INTRODUCTION

The ancient Greeks (some of whom you know were great artists) used the same word for "drawing" as they did for "writing." It made good sense, really. When we draw we are actually saying with lines and smudges on paper what we know and think about the shapes, movement, strength, or weakness — and a lot of other things — of the person, animal, or object we are trying to draw.

In this book I have written and drawn the ideas and methods which have helped me and which I believe will help you to say whatever it is you want to say with drawing. These ideas and methods have been used by good and great artists for generations. I do not promise that they will make you a great artist. For that you need a great talent. But I expect they will help you to draw with some confidence. And if you do have talent, they can help you to become the great artist you want to be.

THE SHAPES OF THINGS

Just about anything you see has its own special shape. And that special shape is made up of smaller shapes. They are the most important reason why things look the way they do. When you make a drawing of something, you are really drawing its main shape and the smaller shapes that are part of it. Therefore, the first thing you need to learn is to see and know these shapes.

DRAWING THE SHAPES

Have you ever noticed that the drawings of most beginners look flat and unreal? That is because the young artists have drawn only the outlines of shapes. They have given them only two dimensions, or measurements — the height and the width. What is lacking is the depth, or thickness, of the shape. We call it the third dimension, and good artists always try to draw it along with the other two dimensions.

There are many ways of drawing the three dimensions of a shape. Here is one that has been used by many great artists for thousands of years. First look carefully at the object you want to draw. Try to see the large shapes that make up that object. When you think you know what they are, take a broad pencil, a crayon, or a piece of charcoal, and go to work.

26

8

STUDYING SHAPES

On the opposite page I have drawn a number of shapes of different things. Take a colored pencil and try to copy them. But don't try too hard! Be brave! Be free! Scribble or smudge away until you have the shape you want. Forget about neatness.

Remember that you are practicing drawing now, not making something to hang on the wall. Use cheap but strong paper that will not tear or crumble as you work. Ordinary wrapping paper is as good as any. Draw quickly, and don't worry about the lines you draw. Scribble or smudge the shapes down any old way, so long as you get them down. Try using the side of your crayon, or the broad side of your pencil or charcoal. Use your thumb or your fingers to smudge the shapes onto the paper. And keep thinking about the thickness of the shapes you are drawing.

You can work on large or small sheets of paper. Keep a pad in your pocket and when you see something that interests you, study its shapes and try to scribble them down on your pad. Do it again and again until you have something that satisfies you. Master the shapes before you try to put in any details at all. Artists, even great artists, are always studying the shapes of things around them, scribbling and smudging them down on paper, just for practice.

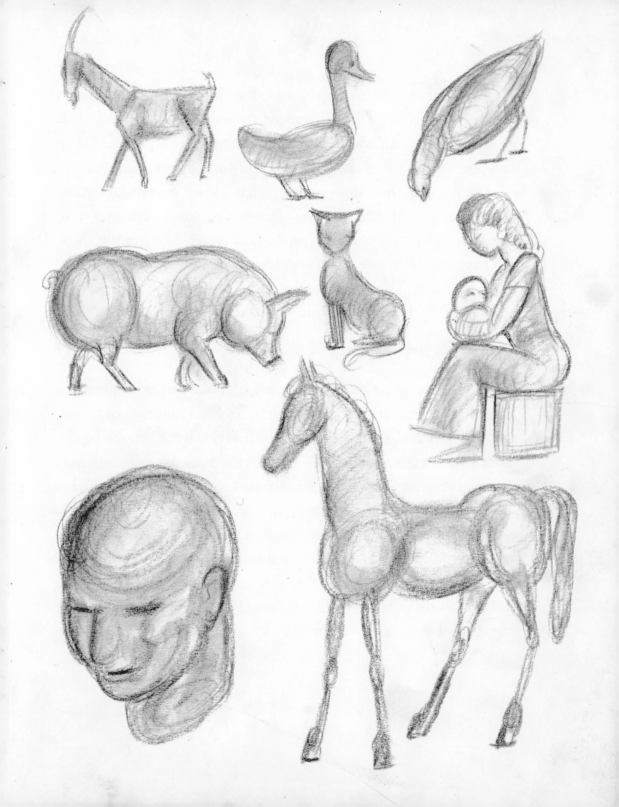

Now, when your shape is as good as you can make it, take a pencil of a different color and surround the shape you have made with a firm line. I used a black line to outline the reddish shapes I scribbled. This method of using one color for studying shapes and a deeper color for doing the final drawing has been in use for thousands of years.

There are still other ways of drawing an object after you have studied it and put its shape on paper. One way is to cover the shape you have scribbled with a sheet of tracing or lightweight typewriter paper and trace it again and again until you are satisfied. Then put down some final lines to surround it and make it definite.

MORE ABOUT SHAPES

There is a great deal more to learn about shapes than can be learned by looking at their outside surfaces. What makes a shape look full, strong, weak, thin, soft, or hard? It is not what you see on the outside, but the inner structure — the skeleton and muscles of the shape. Not only people and animals have skeletons and muscles. Trees, houses — nearly all things — have them.

Four or five hundred years ago such great artists as Leonardo da Vinci and Michelangelo studied the anatomy, or structure, of human beings and animals so thoroughly that they knew more about bones and muscles than did the doctors of those days. Their anatomical drawings are so true that they are used by students of anatomy even today.

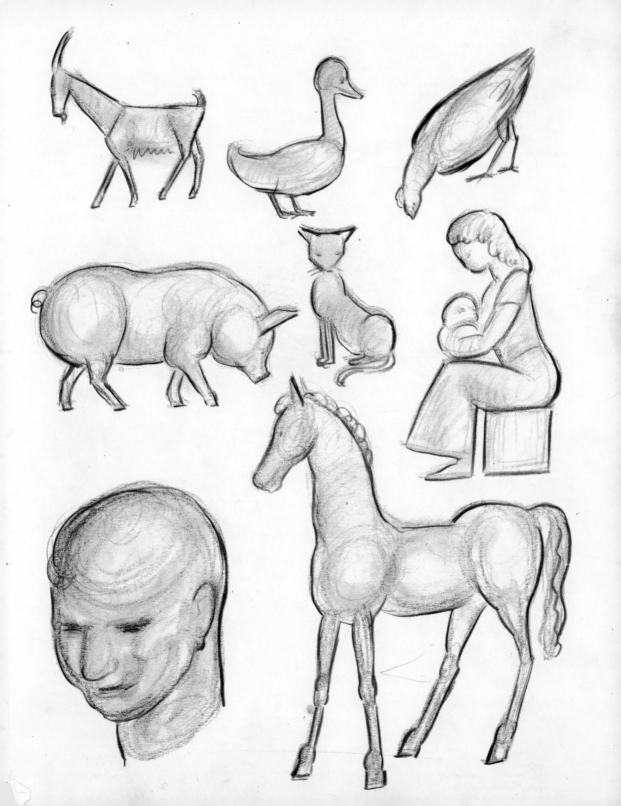

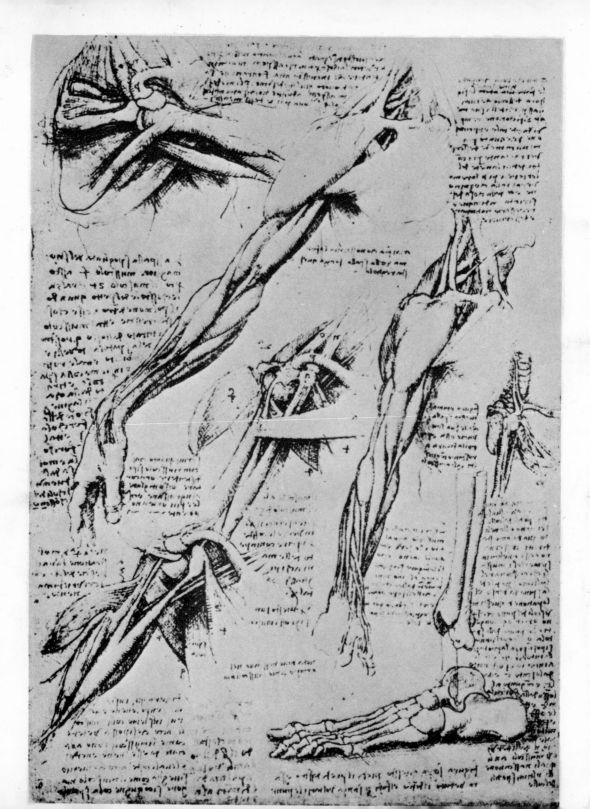

There were — and are — artists who studied the geometric shapes of the subjects they tried to draw. Geometric shapes are cubes, spheres, and things like that. These artists tried to see the shapes without any surface detail at all. Then they built the human figure, or the animal, or whatever it was they were drawing, with cubes, spheres, and other geometric shapes.

I believe that a combination of these two methods — the study of the anatomy of an object and the study of geometric shape — is the best way to develop a sense of the shape of things so that you can make good drawings.

Anatomical drawings by Leonardo da Vinci (1452-1519)

THE HUMAN FIGURE

Let's begin our study of the human figure by looking at the human head. Here are its skeleton and muscle simplified.

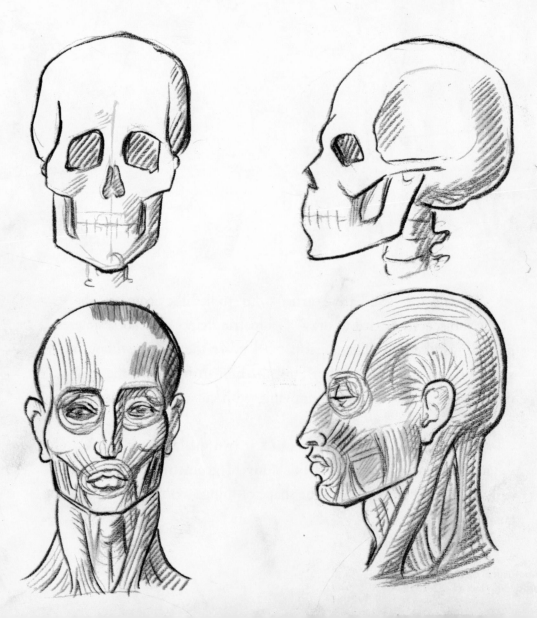

Now here are the general geometric shapes that make up the human head.

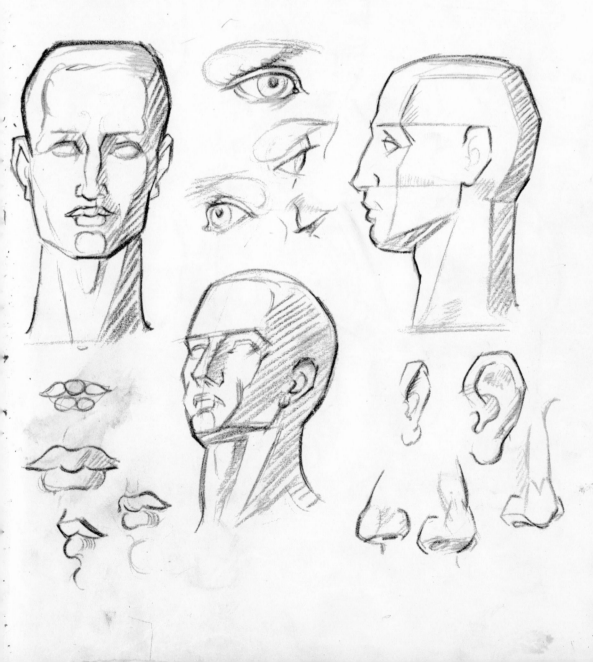

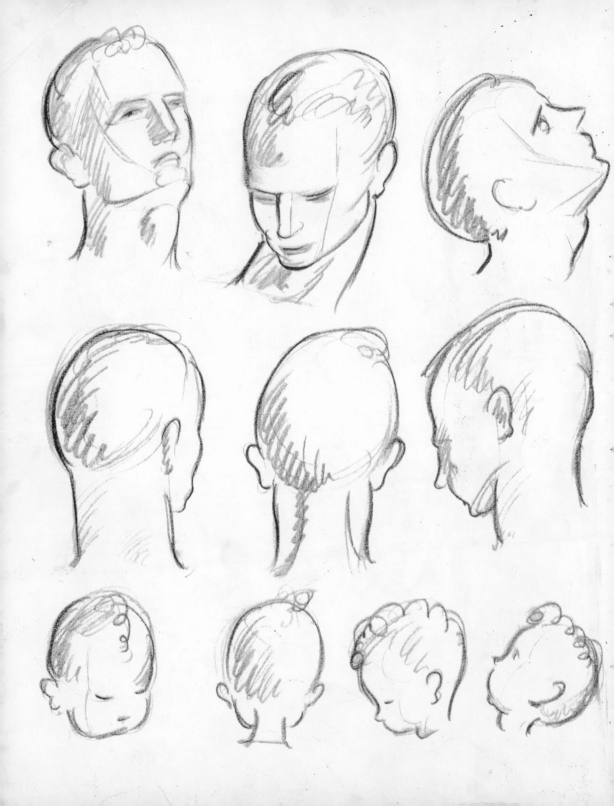

The bones and muscles and geometric shapes are alike in everybody. What, then, makes Mr. Smith look different from Mr. Brown? It is the proportions of his bones and muscles and geometric shapes — their height, width, and thickness — compared to those of Mr. Brown. His color and hair make him look different too.

Albrecht Dürer made charts showing the different proportions of different types of heads. So did Leonardo da Vinci and other great artists.

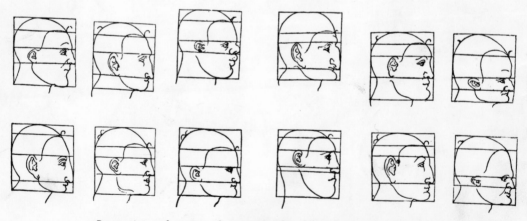

Proportions of various face types, by Albrecht Dürer (1471-1528)

Now let's study the simplified anatomy and geometry of the human figure and of animals.

Men and women differ chiefly in the geometry of their shapes.

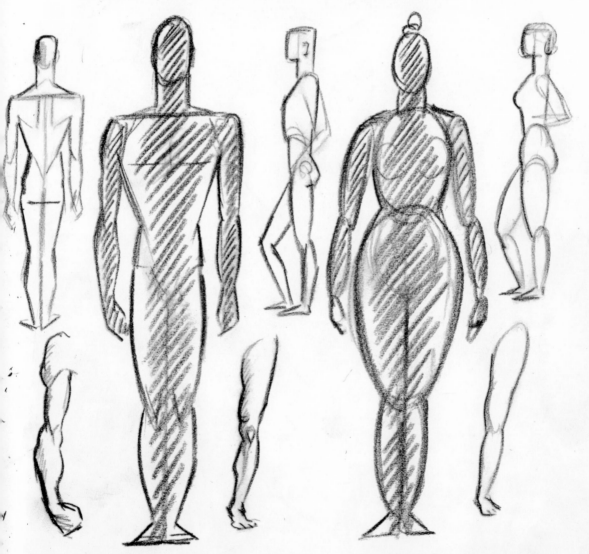

The shapes of a man are usually angular

The shapes of a woman are usually rounder

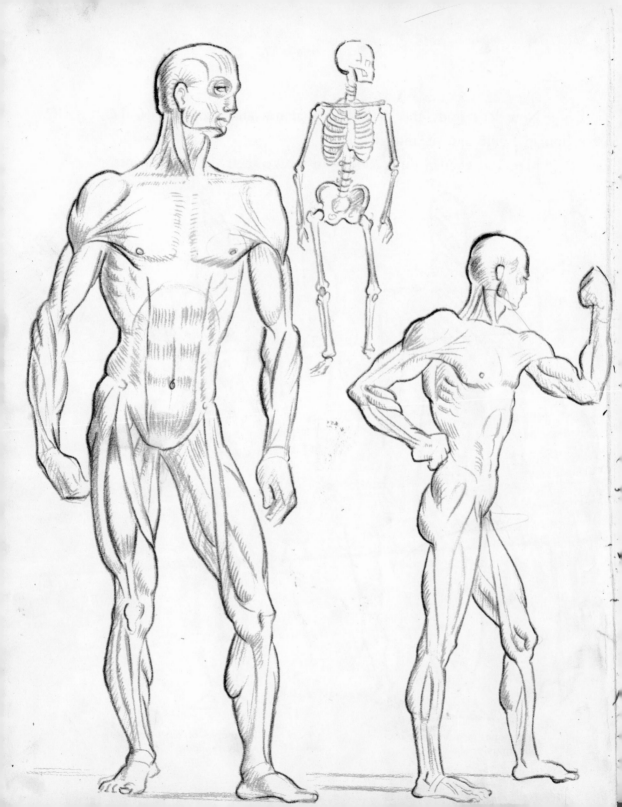

They also differ in the size of their bones and the strength of their muscles. Men's bones are larger, their muscles stronger than those of women.

Women are more delicate and dainty.

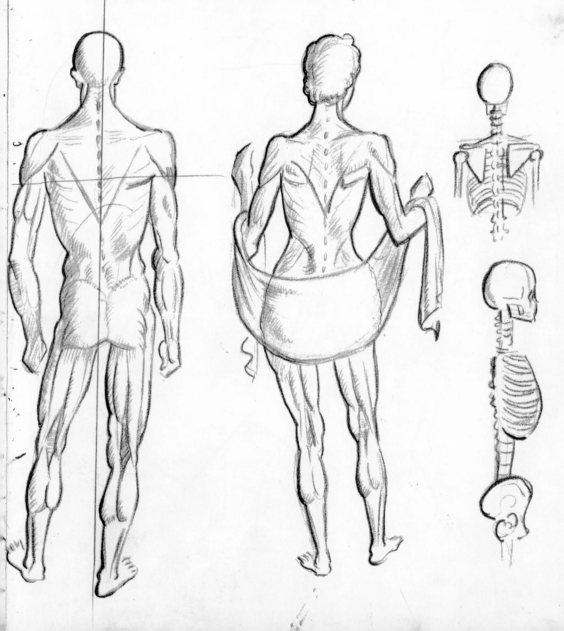

The human spine is made up of twenty-four bones called vertebrae. It bends and twists mainly in the neck and waist. The part of our spine that is attached to our rib basket bends very little when we bend forward or back. The whole spine bends when we bend sidewards.

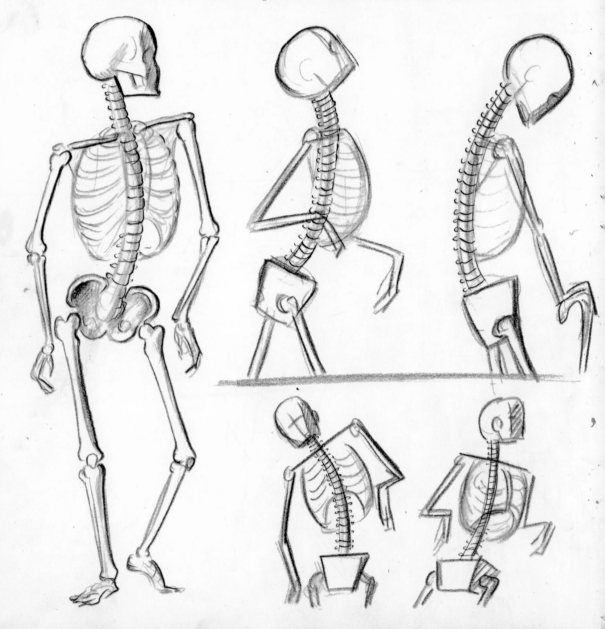

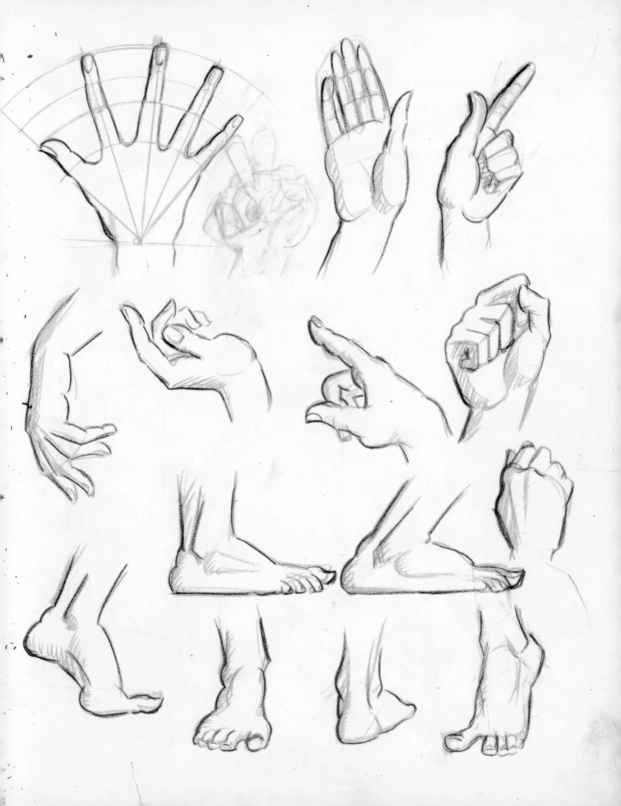

The bones and muscles of children are the same as those of grown-up people. Only the proportions are different.

The average full-grown man is about seven and a half heads high. A tiny baby's head is very large in proportion to the rest of his body. As he grows, that proportion changes.

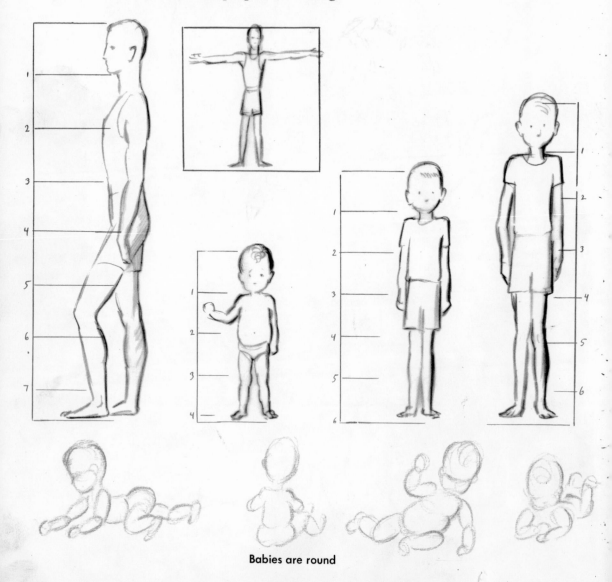

Babies are round

Animals resemble each other in bone and muscle structure. The reason one kind looks different from another is the difference in its proportions and geometric shapes, along with a few other things such as hair growth, horns, tusks, etc

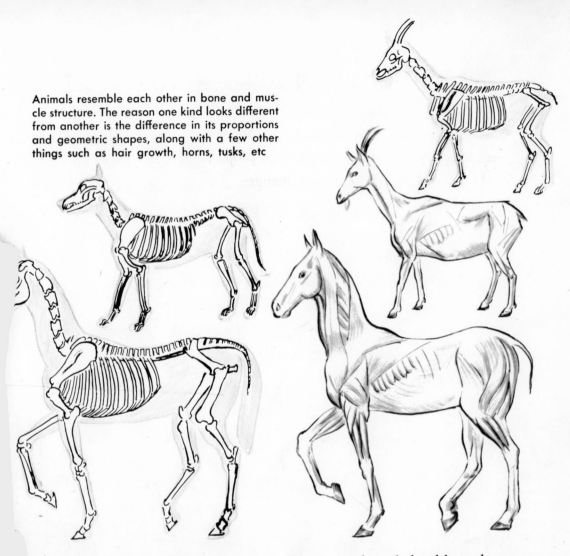

Trees are not feather dusters standing on end, and should not be drawn to look like them. Trees, too, have skeletons. The trunk and branches are the skeleton of a tree.

Do houses have an inner structure? Yes. The frame of a house is its skeleton.

THE MOVEMENT OF SHAPES

Once you have learned to see and know shapes, the next most important thing is learning to see and know the movements of shapes.

Each thing, each person moves in a way all his own. We all walk, but we all walk in our own way. You can recognize a friend by the way he walks, even though he may be in disguise. Animals walk, run, and move each in its own way. Even trees move in their own way as they grow or when the wind tosses them.

Before you start to draw a shape, study the way it moves. Watch the way one shape moves into the shape next to it, the way shapes flow together, the contrasting movements of shapes. Try to feel that movement in your own body. You will draw much better if you feel like the prancing horse or the crouching cat you are trying to get down on paper.

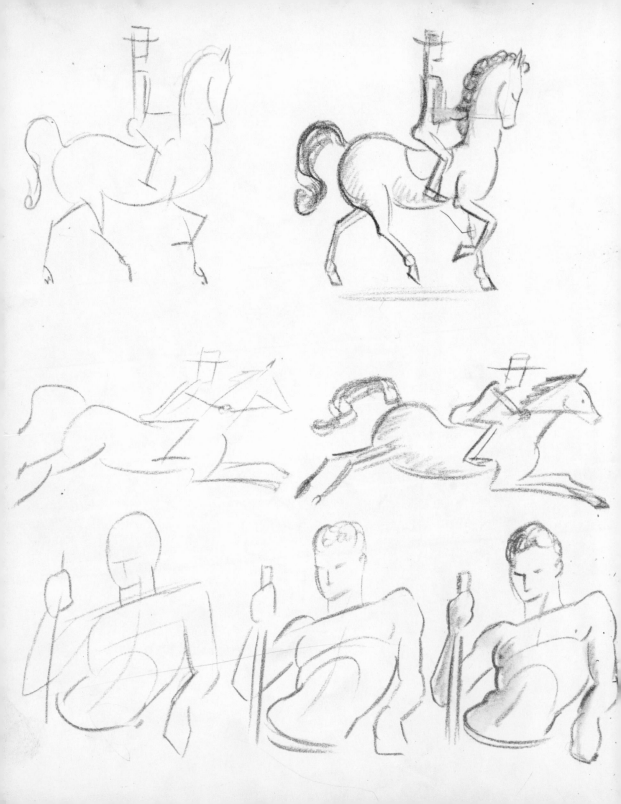

Since the best way to learn how to draw is to draw, why not turn back now and copy some or all of the drawings that you have looked at here? Draw big!

PENCIL DRAWING

If you want to do a finished drawing with a pencil, the first thing to do is to get the right pencil for you and the work you want it to do. Ordinary lead pencils usually have number markings that show how hard or soft they are. No. 1 is a very soft pencil, No. 2 is medium, No. 3 is hard, and No. 4 is very hard.

There are some pencils that have ½ markings on them. I like to use pencils marked 2½. The lines made by softer pencils are apt to smudge as you work, and a harder pencil makes too light a line to suit me. I also like to draw sometimes with an Eagle Veri-thin Black 747 pencil. It gives a good dark line, but it is a little harder to erase than one of the ordinary No. 2½ pencils. When I draw, I usually like to be able to erase.

You will also want a "kneading rubber" — a very soft, pliable rubber — and some heavy bond typewriting paper. That paper has just enough "tooth" or graininess to its surface to catch your pencil strokes well.

Everyone uses a pencil easily and carelessly for writing, doodling, playing tick-tack-toe, etc. But when a beginner starts to draw he usually grips his pencil too tightly. Then he either digs the point into his paper or timidly draws a wavering line as though he were afraid of it.

A pencil will do anything for you provided you don't choke it to death with your fingers!

Hold your pencil just enough to guide it, gently but firmly. Begin by scribbling a little with your wrist resting lightly on your board and your hand holding your pencil lightly. Draw loosely, easily, some rhythmic lines on your paper. Just doodle a bit. Try holding your pencil in different positions in your hand until it works nicely.

Now begin to draw!

Start by lightly whirling in the shape you want to draw. Don't worry about your lines. You have that good kneading eraser in your other fist. Remember that one of the beauties of good drawing is the rhythm and flow of the lines.

When you have some pretty good shapes whirled in, draw your definite surrounding outline.

SHADING (OR MODELING) YOUR DRAWING

The eye of a camera can see and reproduce only the lights and shadows that fall on an object.

But an artist can see and choose those special lights and shadows on an object which will help give his drawing depth and volume. And drawing those lights and shadows is a process that is usually called "shading."

I prefer to call it modeling. To model means to give something form or shape and that is exactly what shading should do. Shading should help give shapes a third dimension. You can, with a little shading, bring forms forward or push them back in your drawing. You can give them a soft round look, or make them look hard and sharp.

The light which falls on the object you are drawing usually comes from only one side and makes shadows on the other side. But there are also many reflecting lights that affect the object you are trying to draw. Do not let any of the natural lights influence your drawing too much. Use light and shadow for your own purposes. You really draw with light as well as with line and shade on your paper. Remember this along with the fact that you are using shading only to give your drawing depth and volume. Then you will not make the mistake of shading your drawing so much that it looks crude and dirty.

To develop the tone or shade around your drawing you can cross-hatch. Hold your pencil lightly, remember.

In drawing lines to shade a form, it is usually best to draw with the movement of the form. But there are times when you can get a better effect by drawing against the movement. Try both methods. You still have that good kneading rubber in your other hand and you can change your drawing.

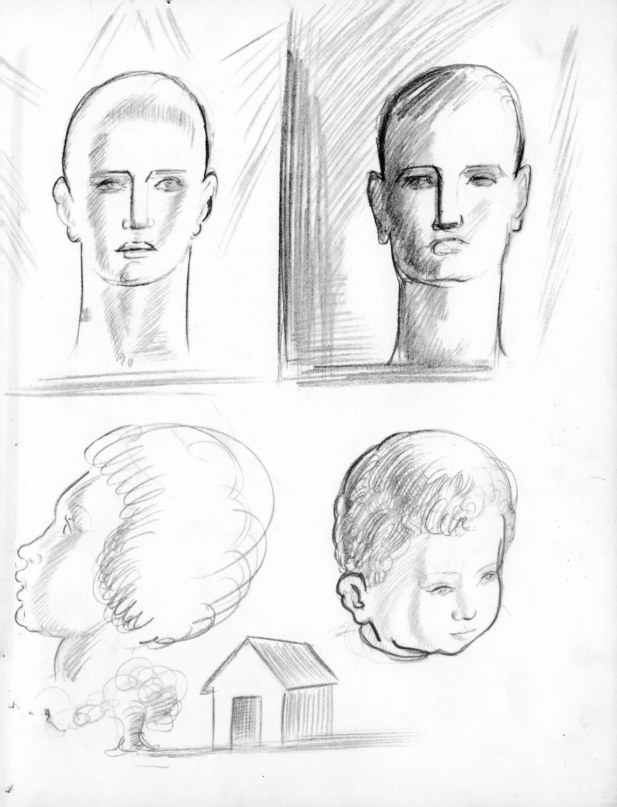

When you put down the final lines surrounding your shapes, use a light line on the side nearest the source of light that falls on the object you are drawing. The outline on the darker side of the object can be drawn with a darker, heavier line. But neither outline should be all dark or all light. The lines should go lightly, then darken to model the forms. Sometimes it is wise to use the darker outline on the lighter side of the object, and the light line on the darker side.

If you want to keep your pencil drawing, use a fixative to fix it to your paper or it will become smudged and rub off. Fixative is a liquid with an alcohol base combined with some sticky substance, perhaps shellac or gum arabic. You blow a thin mist of it through a tube onto your drawing. When the fixative dries your drawing should stay on the paper. Bottles of fixative and small metal tubes used for blowing it are sold in all art supply shops. They are not expensive.

QUALITIES OF PENCIL DRAWING

Each different material with which you draw has its own special quality. Pencil lines can be harsh, or strong, or beautiful and flowing. They can be almost tender. Here are some qualities you should try for in pencil drawing:

three-dimensional shape

good movement

delicate tones

fine, rhythmic, almost poetic lines.

Pencil drawing by Edgar Degas (1834-1917)

Pencil drawing by Jean Auguste Ingres (1780-1867)

PERSPECTIVE

While we still have a pencil in our hands, let's talk a little about perspective. Perspective is a scientific method for drawing things on a flat surface so that they appear to be going back into space.

It is a complicated science, and you do not need to know too much about it right now. You know that things look smaller as they move away from you. You know that parallel lines appear to converge, or come together, as they go off into the distance. I think that is all you need to know at this point in your development.

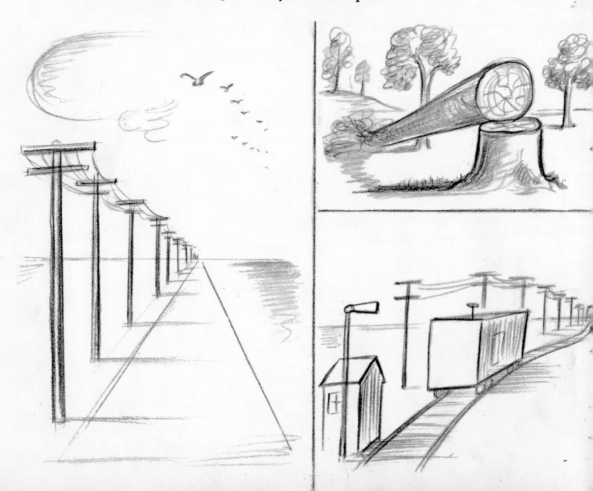

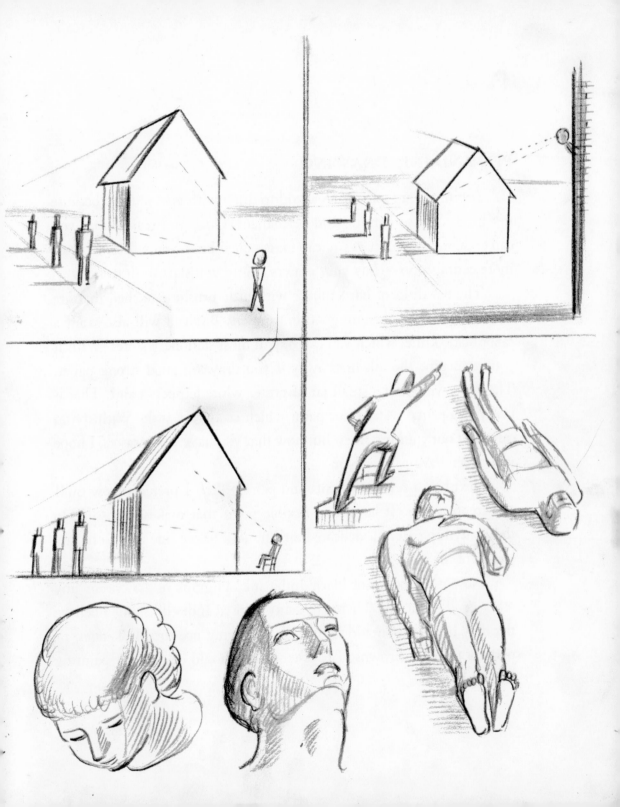

PEN-AND-INK DRAWING

Beginners are sometimes afraid to draw with pen and ink because ink lines seem so definite and permanent. Once you realize that you can erase ink lines just as you can erase pencil lines, you will draw with more courage. So — buy your erasers before you start to draw!

The flat disks of hard rubber with little brushes attached that are used by stenographers are good ink erasers. But you will also want a razor blade knife, which you can buy in most stationery stores. With it you can scrape the ink lines away if you draw on good strong paper. Then you will want a small jar of poster white tempera paint. That is really an opaque water-color paint which costs very little. With it you can paint out your ink lines. But now that you have your erasers, I hope you never have to use them.

Next buy a few pen points and pen holders. I prefer a crow quill pen to any other. It has a fine flexible point that makes it possible to draw anything from a delicate hair line to a heavy line about one sixteenth of an inch wide.

Now get a bottle of black India ink, Higgins or Artone or any other good India ink. There are many colored India inks, but I believe the only ones that should be used for drawing are the black ones, or perhaps the dark browns. The other colors should be used for painting with ink.

Here are lines drawn with four different pen points.

Crow quill   Hawk quill   Ordinary writing pen   Ball point pen

You can use any good paper with a good surface for pen drawing. I prefer a sheet of two-ply Twachtman with either a shiny hot-pressed surface or a kid finish. A hot-pressed surface is smooth, almost polished. A kid finish has just a little tooth or roughness to the surface. A two-ply paper is just about thick enough so that you can erase or scrape out your ink lines.

The smooth surface paper will allow you to move your pen fast. The slightly rough surface paper holds your pen back just a little. I like to work with different kinds of paper, depending on the subject I am drawing and the kinds of lines I want.

You may also use a thinner or heavier paper — a typewriting paper or a Bristol board. And at last get yourself a medium fine water-color brush and a box of paper tissues to clean your pen points.

Now that you have your materials, take a hard lead pencil — number 3 or 2½ — and make an almost complete drawing of some object. Draw lightly, for you will want to erase your pencil lines after you do your pen drawing.

Before you begin drawing with your pen, practice on another clean sheet of paper. Dip your pen in the ink and doodle! Hold your pen a bit more firmly than you do your pencil. Do not dip the point too deep into the ink. Start by making some whirls and swirls, crosshatches, lines of different weight — thin lines, heavy lines, curved lines. Just scribble.

When you feel you can control your pen — draw!

Every line you draw counts when you are using pen and ink. You cannot get the light lines you can with a pencil. Although you can shade your pen drawings in the same way you do your pencil drawings, each pen line, no matter how thin it is, is completely black. There is no in between as there is with a pencil line.

As you shade you can draw lines with your shape or against it. You can crosshatch as you shade, or round out, your shapes. Keep your pen clean by wiping it on your tissue.

When you finish your drawing you can use a brush dipped in ink to put down some completely black areas in the deepest shadows or for some other purpose. But be careful not to use your brush too often or you will be doing a brush drawing.

When your pen drawing is about halfway through and all the most important lines are put down in ink and the ink is dry, erase your pencil lines with a soft kneading rubber, gently. Then go on and finish your pen-and-ink drawing. Do not begin to erase any of your ink lines until you are almost finished with the drawing, because if you erase the ink lines with your hard ink eraser you will find that you scrape the surface of your paper. Then when you draw over the scraped part of the paper the ink lines may blot. Do not draw over the scraped surface of your paper any more than you absolutely have to.

The razor blade knife will also spoil the surface of the paper. And you will have trouble too if you paint out some ink lines with the white poster paints and try to draw on top of the dried paint.

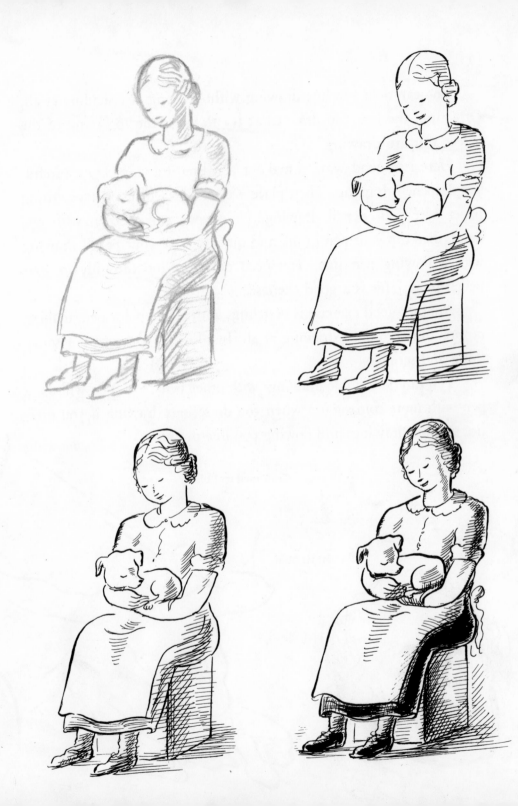

You can do a pen line drawing without using any shading at all. Of course, the line you draw must try to stress the modeling of the object you are drawing.

Here is a good way to make a pen line drawing. Do a careful, simple pencil drawing. Then place a clean sheet of good typewriting paper over your pencil drawing. Hold your paper down with one hand, then dip your pen in ink and quickly trace your pencil drawing with a flowing pen line. You need not stick too carefully to your pencil lines. This is a good exercise.

Another good exercise is sketching with a ball point pen, making no preliminary pencil drawing at all. Just look at someone or something and scribble.

You can do scribble drawings with other pens, too. You will use a pen with more competence when you do serious drawing if you practice scribble drawings and flowing pen line drawings.

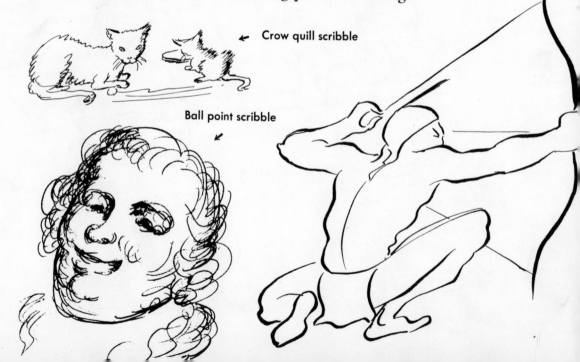

← Crow quill scribble

Ball point scribble

QUALITIES OF INK DRAWING

Here are the qualities you should try for in pen-and-ink drawing:
    three-dimensional shape
    good movement
    fine rhythm of line.

You must use your ink wisely or you will just have another cluttered, muddy drawing. Ink drawings should be crisp, uncluttered. Each line or ink blot must mean something. Use less rather than more ink to get this effect.

Scribble pen drawing by Honoré Daumier (1808-1879)

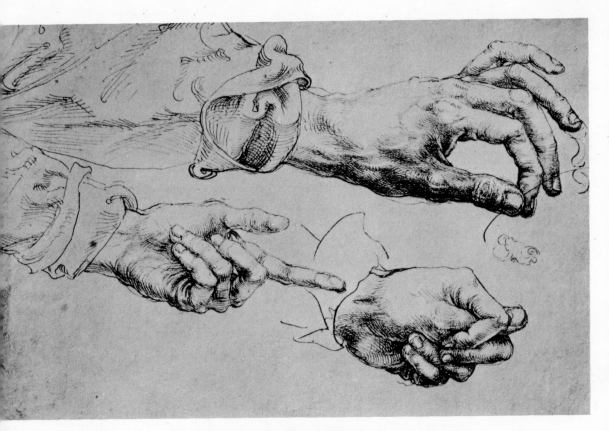

Pen drawing by Albrecht Dürer

CHARCOAL AND PASTEL DRAWING

The techniques used in drawing with charcoal, pastels, and dry crayon are very much alike. Often all three of these materials are used in the same drawing.

Charcoal is charred wood. Sticks of charcoal are sold in every art supply shop. You can even make your own if there is no art shop in your neighborhood.

Pastels are dry, brittle sticks of different-colored chalks.

When you plan to do a drawing with charcoal or pastel, the first thing to consider is the paper you use. There is a special paper sold for drawing with charcoal. The same paper can be used for pastel drawing. It is a slightly rough paper with a ribbed, grained surface. But charcoal can be used with almost any paper that has a slightly rough surface. There is also a special paper made for use with pastels. This paper has a sandy surface. It is like a very fine sandpaper. Both charcoal and pastel papers come in various colors.

Both charcoal and pastel can be used with a lot of freedom. You can use your fingers to smudge in the shadows and tones as you model your shapes. You can also use charcoal and pastel in the same way you use a pencil. And you can use your kneading rubber to erase or pick out the lights on the tops and sides of the forms. These lights are called highlights. They help to make your forms look fuller.

After you have finished a charcoal or pastel drawing you will have to use a fixative to fix it to your paper. If you do not, it will rub or flake off.

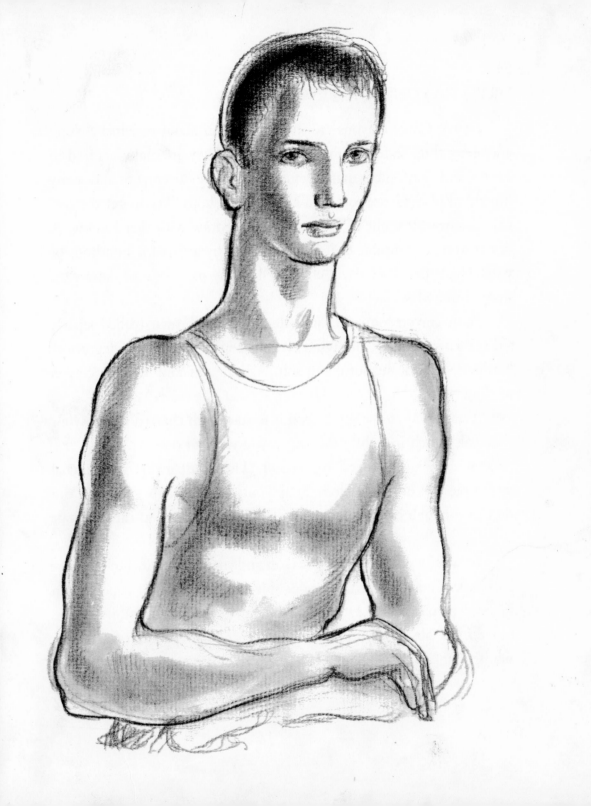

DRY CRAYON DRAWING

Dry or Conte crayons are sticks of crayon about two inches long and about three sixteenths of an inch wide. They are manufactured in France and Conte is the manufacturer's name. Conte crayons and many imitations of them are sold in all art supply shops. Try to get the real Conte crayon. It is one of the best things to draw with that I know. A dry crayon very similar to it has been used by artists for hundreds of years. Conte dry crayon will cling well to any paper except those with shiny polished surfaces.

Conte crayon comes in four colors — black, brown (called sepia), red (called sanguine), and white. It comes in three different degrees of hardness — hard, medium, and soft. Ask for a medium Conte crayon to draw with.

A good way to use dry crayon is to start with charcoal. With your charcoal, sketch in lightly the object you want to draw. Just give it a general shape and general movement. Then dust away the charcoal with a piece of dry clean cloth. Snap your cloth at the paper when you do this. Enough of the charcoal will remain so that you can see your sketch.

Now take your red Conte crayon and snap it in half. Holding the half stick of crayon so that the wide side of it rests on your paper, begin to develop your shapes. Draw lightly at first, then more definitely. You can do just about anything with Conte crayon. You can draw fine sensitive lines with the edge of the crayon, crosshatch, smudge in deep

tones, or model over your paper with your fingers. You will enjoy working with these crayons.

You can develop your drawing further by putting down your final lines with black Conte crayon. Then, after you have used your kneading rubber to pick out shapes and highlights, you can use a smudge of the white Conte to sharpen the highlights.

You can also lay out your main masses or shapes with charcoal and round them out with some light-colored pastel. And then you can put down your final lines with Conte crayon. But this drawing must also be fixed, so use your fixative. It would be wise to use fixative even on straight Conte crayon drawings, for they can be smudged with careless handling.

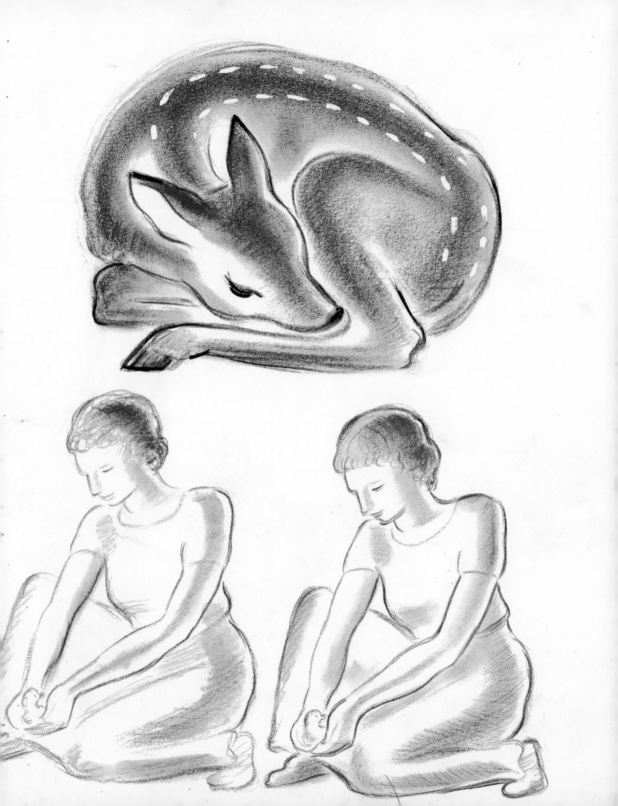

Red crayon drawing by Michelangelo (1475-1564)

QUALITIES OF DRY CRAYON, PASTEL, OR CHARCOAL DRAWING

Dry crayon, pastel, or charcoal drawings, or a combination of all three, should have about the same qualities as any other drawing. But the first quality these drawings must have is fine, full shape — good three-dimensional shape. If your drawing does not have it, tear it up, throw it away, and start over again!

BRUSH DRAWING

After you have practiced drawing with pencils, charcoal, crayon, etc., for a good long time, and believe you have the results you want, be brave and try a brush drawing. You must really know how to draw before you can expect to get any results with a brush.

There are a number of ways of drawing with a brush;

(1) drawing directly with a brush, using ink or a deep black water color;

(2) drawing with a brush, pen, and a black wash;

(3) drawing with a brush, using a pen and water-color pencil.

Get yourself some good sable water-color brushes ranging in size from a very fine to a half-inch brush. These brushes are expensive, but they are worth the money. Also get a couple of bamboo-handled Chinese brushes if you can. You will want your India ink, and also a tube of lampblack water color or a tube of ivory-black water color, a jar of white tempera poster paint, and a water-color pencil.

You can use almost any good paper with a grainy surface for brush drawings — water-color papers, charcoal papers, boards, or heavy typewriting paper. If you use a very thin paper for brush drawings the paper may wrinkle and buckle as the ink or water-color wash dries.

DRAWING DIRECTLY WITH A BRUSH

First make a light pencil sketch of your object, a very simple, flowing line drawing. Then point your brush. To do this, dip your brush in water, then, with a whirling twist, snap the water out. The hairs of the brush will come to a point at the tip. Or you can point your brush by twirling it between your wetted lips.

Now dip the pointed brush into your ink or black water-color and practice a few brush strokes on another sheet of paper. Quickly and easily draw lines that vary from extremely thin to thick. When you think you have gained some control over the brush, dip it again in ink or water color and begin to draw.

Draw quickly and boldly. Don't be timid. Try to think of the shape, movement, and everything else you want to get into your drawing, all at the same time. Try to get it all down with just a few swoops of your brush. The pencil lines are only guide lines. You do not have to follow them exactly with your brush.

Use only white tempera poster paint to correct or erase all types of brush drawings. Be sure your ink or your water-color brush drawing is thoroughly dry before you use your white paint. And do not use too much of the white paint.

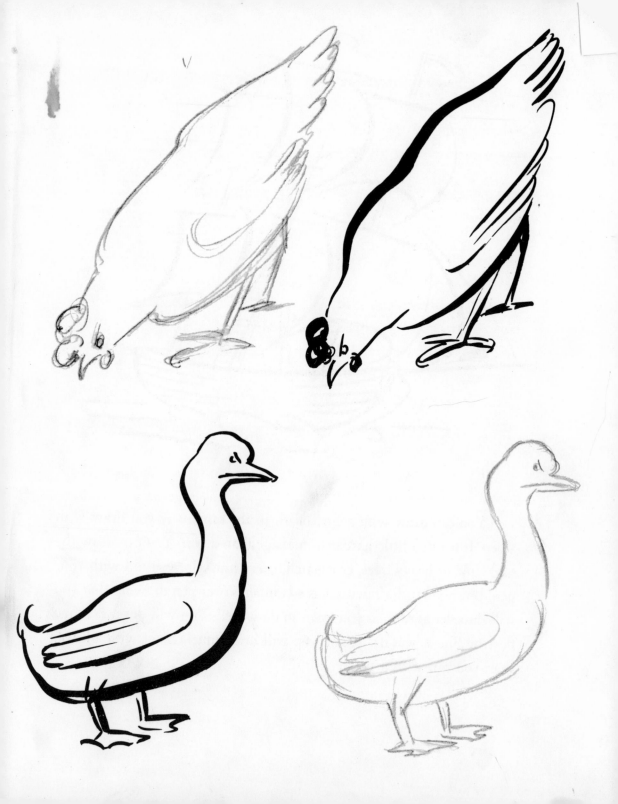

You can draw with a fine brush in the same way you draw with a pen. It is just a little harder to manage than a pen. You can draw the same fine or heavy lines, crosshatch, everything else you did with your pen. But fine brush drawing has advantages over pen drawing that you will discover as soon as you learn to do it well. You will develop a fine flowing line as you draw, and you will draw much faster with a brush than you can with a pen.

WASH AND PEN DRAWINGS

You can get interesting effects by combining pen line and wash. After you have made a quick pen drawing, wash in your shades and model your drawing with a wet brush.

Do a very light pencil drawing. Then put a little black water color and water in one glass, and some clean clear water in another. Now get your pen and ink and quickly draw over your light pencil drawing. Then just the second the ink begins to dry, wet your brush in the clear water and wash over your pen line, putting in the shadows and modeling your drawing. If some of the ink is too dry and will not mix with the clear water, dip your brush in the black water-color wash and then do your shadows and modeling. You can sharpen your drawings at the end with a few well-placed pen lines.

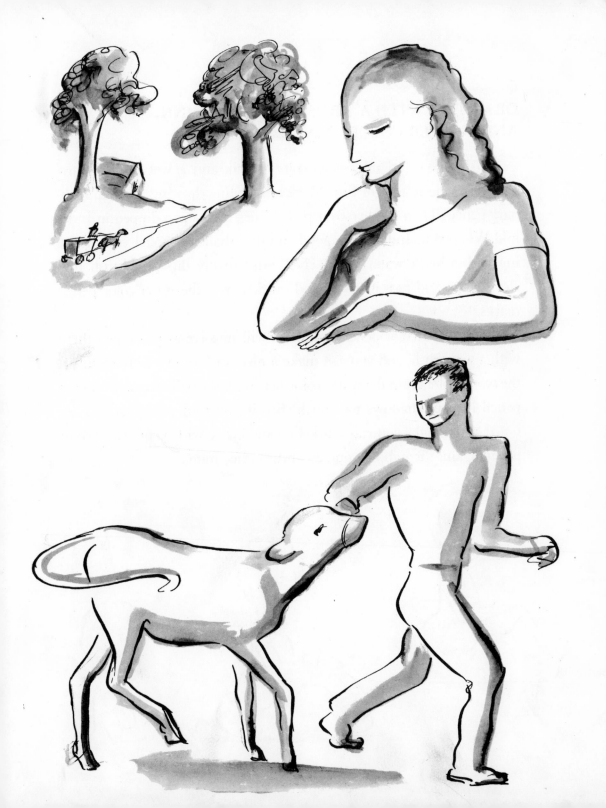

DRAWING WITH A BRUSH, PEN AND INK, AND WATER-COLOR PENCIL

Using pen and ink, water-color pencil, and a wet brush in the same drawing is a lot of fun. Make a light line drawing with an ordinary pencil. Then go over your pencil lines with a pen dipped in India ink. When your India ink is good and dry, shade or model your drawing with a black water-color pencil. And finally dip your brush into clean water and pass it wisely and quickly over the water-color pencil marks.

The water-color pencil markings will dissolve as you touch them with a wet brush, and you can make a nice wash drawing. Remember, the water color from the water-color pencil marks will spread, so do not pencil in your shadows too much. But if you find your shadows are not dark enough, you can mark in some black with your water-color pencil again, then apply your wet brush once more.

NOW — PRACTICE!

Now that we have come to the end of this book, here is the most important thing to remember: a good artist practices even more than a good athlete. He practices constantly by drawing and drawing and drawing. So, if you want to be a good artist — draw!

Draw everything or anything you see around you. Ask your relatives or friends to sit quietly in a good light while you try to draw their heads or hands. Draw your pets. Make a lot of scribbled sketches of them, and make careful drawings of them too. It is all good practice.

A good exercise is to copy the drawings of great artists. Your public library has books with reproductions of beautiful drawings by the greatest artists who ever lived. Find them, and copy the drawings.

When a good artist is not drawing he can exercise and practice by just looking at things and studying them. As you walk along the street or the road, look at people, animals, and the things around you. Study their shapes and their movements. Think how you could put their shapes and movements down on paper. That's a good exercise, and a lot of fun. When you get home try to put them down on paper. That's the best exercise of all.

So — draw, draw, draw, just for fun, or to become a great artist.

INDEX